SURVIVING A TSUNAMI

And Other Storms of Life

Teddy Butler Copeland

SURVIVING A TSUNAMI

Lambert Book House
4139 Parkway Drive
Florence, Alabama 35630

© 2008, Lambert Book House

All rights reserved. No part of this publication may be reproduced, stored in a retrieval system, or transmitted in any form or by any means—electronic, mechanical, photocopy, recording, or any other—except for brief quotations in printed reviews, without the prior permission of the publisher.

Scripture taken from *The Message*. Copyright 1993, 1994, 1995, 1996, 2000, 2001, 2002. Used by permission of NavPress Publishing Group.

Published by
Lambert Book House
4139 Parkway Drive
Florence, Alabama 35630

ISBN 978-0-89315-428-8
Printed in the United States of America

TABLE OF CONTENTS

Dedication 5

Introduction 6

1. HOW IT HAPPENED 9

2. LANDING ON YOUR FEET 19

3. LIFE JUST KEEPS COMING AT YOU 27

4. THE LESSON OF BABY GIRAFFES 37

5. THERE ARE NO DOGS 47

6. BELOW THE WATERLINE 59

7. SEEING THE SHORE 69

8. GOD WITH US IN THE FIRE 77

9. NO PAT FORMULAS 87

10. THE CYCLE OF COMFORT 95

11. HOW YOU FINISH 105

12. A RAINBOW PROMISE 115

13. TYING A KNOT 123

Concluding Activity 133

Dedication

To Cathy Spivey, my big sister
I still want to be like you when I grow up!

To Linda Williams
Webster could define "generous" by putting your name next to it.

To Norm Curington
Your friendship is one of our family's greatest treasures.

*Special thanks
to Rick Von Feldt*

Introduction

They were friends from college, old acquaintances we hadn't seen in years. Despite good intentions to the contrary, we'd lost touch shortly after graduation.

Then, unexpectedly, while visiting a church in another city, we ran into one another. An initial flurry of recognition was followed by hugs and handshakes, the inevitable catching up. You know, condense the last twenty years of your life into three brief sentences.

Probably we went first, eager to tell of accomplishments and God's goodness. Mission work, great kids, law school, a few books published.

Our friends listened quietly, smiling, until we paused. And what had they been up to? we inquired.

The husband stroked his beard, choosing his words very deliberately. "We've survived a tsunami," he sighed. And somehow I knew he wasn't referring to a recent catastrophe in Asia.

Full of emotion, our friends went on to tell of a year of crisis in the lives of the children they'd adopted. They spoke of startling blasts of trouble which had come without warning, of the struggle to maintain footing amidst the tremors, of how they'd learned—and were still in the process of learning—to cling only to what is solid and immovable.

Since our conversation that day, I've thought often of this analogy. All of us, at one time or another, have circumstances in life that hit us hard, knock us over. A tidal wave sweeps in, perhaps one we didn't even know was coming.

How do we react? What do we do?

Can we survive a tsunami? If so, how?

"As we drove, I was on my computer, working on my annual year-in-review document. How odd, now, to remember what I was thinking: 'What in 2004 will be my most memorable event?' Little did I know it {was yet to} happen . . . ."

—Rick Von Feldt,
written concerning December 25, 2004,
the day before the tsunami

"Our whole lives are divided into before Tom died and after Tom died."

—from "Who Financed 9/11?"
October 2005 Reader's Digest
Quote by sister of Tom Burnett, killed in
the crash of Flight 93 in a Pennsylvania
field on September 11, 2004

Chapter 1

"They suspected nothing until the flood hit and swept everything away."

—*Luke 17:27*
The Message

How It Happened

At first, the ocean pulled back. It was as if somewhere, way out at sea, a god pulled a plug on the bathtub. The water was sucked backwards, leaving only a muddy, potholed ground, full of flopping fish and small holes of water.

All of the seniors and families (mostly the ones on the beach at 9:00 in the morning) decided it was a great time to explore this unique moment. They walked out and looked at the new landscape. They explored trinkets never seen before, as this part of the ocean bed had never been exposed in fifty years. Children bounced along to little pools of water, newly created . . . perfect for jumping in. Others slept on the beach, taking in the cool and pleasant morning air.

Then, you saw it. The horizon began to be blocked out . . . a dark, blue-black wall sprang to life. You could tell the water was coming back.

It felt odd. You wondered, "Why is this happening?" But no logical reason came to mind. There was a full moon last night, so perhaps the moon was creating an abnormal tide. Most of us didn't live by the ocean, so we had no clue how the ocean was really supposed to work.

1 SURVIVING A TSUNAMI — How It Happened

Many locals stood by the retaining wall. They knew the power of the ocean, and, like a man who had once been bitten by a snake, were fearful to get any closer.

But there were fish—large, flopping fish—lying there. Perfect for frying or baking. How could you just let them lie there? And so a few locals came out to explore. And if the locals were out there, then surely they must know what was happening. So surely it must be safe . . . .

But then we saw the wall. At first {it was} way out at sea. But, wait. If you blinked your eyes, it changed positions really fast. For a few seconds, everyone was mesmerized by the wall. And the sound. Then, with the snap of a finger, hundreds were popped out of their hypnosis. People started to walk. Fast. And then run. And soon, everyone started to scream. "Get up on the wall!" some shouted.

The moment of revelation arrives. A tsunami sweeps in, knocking the ground right out from under our feet, and life will never–ever–be the same.

The water filled up the beach like a gorging bathtub. Water came at people 150 miles an hour. And no matter how hard you tried, unless you were close to the wall, you couldn't outrun it.

Some people stumbled. Some held their ground or were swept with the water towards the wall. People sputtered and coughed. Some went down.

Most were in shock to have seen such a thing happen.

But that was only the beginning. Many people were able to stand back up again, bruised and battered, or having had all of their clothing ripped off. But it wasn't over.

The second swell came, and this one was the life-taking swell. Larger. Fiercer. Taller by ten feet, it pushed hard and strong.

In ten seconds {everything} was washed away.

And the people? Few had a real chance. Even if you could swim, the items being thrown about, above and underneath, battered you. Glass from storefronts cut you.

People talk of two waves. The incoming wave was tough. But once the water from the second wave pulled back, everything floating in that water had to fall. Half of it flowed back out to sea, like the hand of a monster grabbing and not letting go. The rest fell to the ground as the water vacated. Debris stacked three feet high covered everything. And the rest just washed out to sea, only to be returned each morning, little by little.

And all the while, morning sunshine warmed the day.

> —First-hand account of tsunami by Rick Von Feldt who was on Patong Beach in Phuket on the morning of December 26, 2004

One moment can change everything.

It may be a phone call. A doctor's diagnosis. A police officer at your door.

Words are uttered that one's brain cannot—will not—comprehend. The room starts to spin; a heart nearly stops.

I'm pregnant, says your daughter.

I've found someone else, says your spouse.

The business is bankrupt, admits a partner. *All savings are depleted.*

The moment of revelation arrives. A tsunami sweeps in, knocking the ground right out from under our feet, and life will never—ever—be the same.

* * *

In the 1998 movie, *Hope Floats,* Sandra Bullock plays Bertie, a former beauty queen who appears on national television for what she has been led to believe is a makeover.

Instead, fictional talk-show host Toni Post (whose motto is "Getting down and dirty with real people") surprises her by bringing out Bertie's husband, Billy, and her best friend, Connie . . . and reveals that the two are having an affair.

The camera moves in for a close-up of Bertie's shock, horror and disbelief.

Talk about a tsunami.

Granted, most real-life disasters don't hit in quite as dramatic fashion as those dreamed up by Hollywood.

Still, most lives have moments equally devastating and, even without a television camera to record it, the effects can be crushing.

Elizabeth Edwards, wife of Senator John Edwards, has written a book called *Saving Graces* about what has to be the worst horror a mother can face: the loss of a child. Her teenage son Wade was killed in a car accident on the way to the beach for spring break when he was 16. Writing of the "unwanted present" that comes to bereaved parents, she says, "I had the strange gift of knowing that nothing will ever be as bad as that. The worst day of my life had already come."

Listen to this description from Psalm 107 of what happens when a storm hits. (It sounds almost like a ride on a roller coaster!)

1 SURVIVING A TSUNAMI — How It Happened

> *You shot high in the sky,*
> *then the bottom dropped out;*
> *your hearts were stuck in your throats.*
> *You were spun like a top,*
> *you reeled like a drunk,*
> *you didn't know which way was up.*
> —verses 26,27
> **The Message**

That's a lot of mixed metaphors, but it captures the helplessness one feels when the storms of life hit. It's like being in an automobile on an icy highway, spinning out of control, and not able to do anything to make it stop.

When we were in college, my husband was in an improvisational group called Pied Pipers which performed for children. One of their routines was "Let's Go on a Bear Hunt," a chant which one person led with everyone else echoing. You journeyed (using hand motions) through all kinds of places—a swamp, dark woods, a lake—with this key line: "Can't go over it, can't go around it, let's go through it." And there you went: *swish, swish, swish* or *splash, splash, splash*, making your way along. You got bitten by chiggers, chased by a bull, covered in cockleburs, and it was a lot of fun for kids because it was make-believe.

In the real world, as adults, we have to face things that are intimidating and challenging, and often it's no fun at all because the situations are real. How much better it would be, how much easier, if we could go around these obstacles, get away from them or avoid them altogether. But we can't. Our purpose in this book is to discuss how to make it *through* all the things that we encounter.

FOR THOUGHT AND DISCUSSION

- Think of a time in your life when you were hit by a tsunami.

- What are the similarities between figurative and literal storms?

- Why do you think current society is so obsessed with the life storms of celebrities?

- What kind of storms divide our lives into "Before" and "After"?

🌋 What personal goals would you like to accomplish in this study of storms?

🌋 Share with others a passage which has helped you through a personal time of crisis.

Notes

Chapter 2

"Everyone is waking up
to the reality of
what happened.
The shock is wearing off,
and everyone is
trying to deal with it."

—*Rick Von Feldt*

Landing on Your Feet

The novel, *Queen of the Underworld* by Gail Godwin, features a character named Tess. Tess is a very resourceful figure, and she attributes her strength to something which happened to her as a child. When she was twelve years old, she survived a horrible hurricane in Florida where she lived. It was 1926 (back in the days, she notes, before they started giving hurricanes a name). Tess's mother sent her to the hardware store for a rake to clean up the debris in their yard because she thought the hurricane had passed. Instead, though, they were in the calm eye of it. Walking along, Tess was suddenly lifted off the sidewalk and blown nearly three blocks down the street. Listen to how she describes it:

There I was, flying through the air
along with coconuts and roof shingles and blowing sand.
I looked down and saw a grand piano and some oriental rugs
floating down the street on top of the water.
Then my feet were on the ground again
and I had my arms around this big old royal palm
and I held on for dear life until the turbulence was past.
Just think of it. One hundred and thirteen people
were drowned or crushed in that hurricane,
but I landed on my feet.

Could something like that really happen? I don't know. If you've ever read actual accounts from tornadoes or hurricanes, you know that strange things do take place. But regardless of the story's validity, let's use Tess's description of her experience to consider an important question.

How can we "land on our feet" after a storm? How do we survive?

I believe it's important for us to consider this topic because storms are inevitable. Like it or not, at some point in our lives they're going to come.

When our family lived in Brazil in the 1980's, I never remember any thunder or lightning in the area where we lived. Oh, we had rain (lots of it during the rainy season in the years there wasn't a drought), but no electrical storms. I'm no meteorologist, so I'm not sure why that was the case. Maybe it had something to do with the fact that Fortaleza, our city of residence, was very close to the equator.

How can we "land on our feet" after a storm? How do we survive?

There may be certain places in the world where few storms occur. But in life, there's no such safe haven.

No matter who you are, no matter where you live, some type of turbulence will find you.

In Job 14:1 we read, "Man that is born of woman is of few days, and full of trouble." Notice it doesn't say, "You may have some trouble along the way" or "It could possibly happen if you run into some bad luck." No. It says, very matter-of-factly, life is "full of trouble." Period. In other words, it's a given, a cold hard reality from which no one is exempt.

I recently wrote some Vacation Bible School material for fifth and sixth graders. (That's a difficult age. You couldn't pay me to go back and be twelve years old again. You also couldn't pay me to go back and be a substitute teacher for that age again! Middle school's tough.) One of the lessons in this particular series was on Esther. So, in thinking about that being a time in young people's lives full of angst and anxiety and a time when they begin comparing themselves to others (usually in an unfavorable way), one of the points I made was this: On the surface, Esther probably seemed like a golden girl. To those around her, more than likely, it appeared she had it made. Wouldn't you agree? Let's face it, she was obviously gorgeous. She came in first place in the king's beauty pageant! She got to be queen, live in a palace, have servants. Who wouldn't want to be her?

Yet Esther had a great sorrow. She'd had a tragedy in her life. She lost both her parents—we're not sure how or when—but apparently when she was very young. So her life wasn't as problem-free as it may have looked to others.

And that is so often the case with people around us. We may not know their pain; it may not always be visible. But that doesn't mean it isn't there.

A friend told me once, "If you think people haven't had a major crisis in their life, there are two explanations. Either they're very young, or else you just don't know them as well as you think you do."

Ruth Graham has it right in her book title: *There's A Broken Heart In Every Pew*.

Since storms are going to come and going to come to everyone, we, like Tess, need something to hang onto until they pass. Nothing can give us greater stability than God's Word.

The Bible is full of storms—literal and figurative—which nearly swept some folks away. Consider the following:

The flood (Genesis 6-8). Nothing like that had ever happened! Noah and his family had never even seen rain before, so imagine how hard it was to deal with. Sometimes when our life storms hit, they are like nothing we've ever experienced.

Sodom and Gomorrah (Genesis 19). Sin brings about many of the storms in life. There's no way to ever account for the damage it leaves behind.

Hailstorm in the 10 plagues (Exodus 9). Wouldn't it be great if today—like back then—storms only hit the enemies of God and we, His people, were protected? Unfortunately, that's not the case anymore.

Contest with Baal (1 Kings 18). The text says that the sky became black with clouds. In a similar way, life storms can shroud our spirits with depression.

Jonah (Jonah 1:3-17). Some storms are of our own making!

The wise and foolish builders (Matthew 7:24-27). Storms can sweep us away if we're not well grounded.

Storm on the sea (Matthew 8:23-27). Scripture says the boat was "covered with waves." That's how we may feel in the midst of a life storm—as though we're drowning. Oh, and don't we wish Jesus would just do like He did in this particular instance: say "Peace, be still" and make it all go away?

Paul's shipwreck (Acts 27 NKJV). "Neither sun nor stars appeared for many days"—an apt description of most life storms!

SURVIVING A TSUNAMI — Landing on Your Feet

FOR THOUGHT AND DISCUSSION

- Look at descriptions (from newspapers or on-line) of actual hurricanes or tornadoes.

- Share these accounts. How do they compare to the effects of life storms?

- Why do people try to hide the fact they're going through storms? Is this a good thing?

- How can we as God's people make it easier to share our difficulties with one another?

- Are some storms better not shared? Why or why not?

- Make a list of things we should hang on to in periods of high wind.

2 SURVIVING A TSUNAMI — Landing on Your Feet

Notes

Chapter 3

> "My life didn't turn out the way I thought it would. And I didn't see it coming. I should have seen it coming."
>
> — Roy Hobbs
> *"The Natural"*

Life Just Keeps Coming At You

In her novel, *Queen of Broken Hearts*, Cassandra King's main character is a family therapist. On the wall of her office she has a poster to which all her clients can relate—a beach scene with big, rough, relentless waves pounding the shore. The slogan underneath confirms: *Life just keeps coming at you.*

A friend of mine who collects quilts counts as some of her most valued items those which have stood the test of such battering. "Sometimes," she explains, tenderly displaying her tattered treasures, "life knocks your stuffing out!"

Recently my husband and I had a brief stay in Montgomery, Alabama. We checked in at a hotel called The Madison (thus named, we determined, because it was surely built in the 1800's when James Madison was president! Not really. But it seemed that way.) The week we were in town, it was undergoing renovations, so several things didn't work . . . like elevators, ice machines, oh, and the ever-important showers. Well, they sort of worked; water came out of the spigot. But every time it did, it was an adventure to say the least. The water started out great, just the temperature you wanted, but then without any warning, it turned ice cold. After a few minutes of that, it became scalding hot. And back and forth it went, alternating between the two. I think I set a new personal record on this trip for fastest time to bathe!

But that's similar to what happens in life. Things are going along great, just the way we want, when all of a sudden, without warning, we're blasted with trouble. A storm hits. And before we get over it, along comes another . . . and another.

New York newspapers once covered the plight of a gentleman named Lawrence Hanratty who was struck with the following tragedies:

- He was nearly electrocuted in a construction site accident that put him in a coma for weeks.
- Two of the lawyers fighting for his liability claim died and a third was disbarred.
- His wife left him.
- He was involved in a car accident, and after police left the scene, he was held up and robbed.
- He faced both heart and liver disease.

3 SURVIVING A TSUNAMI — Life Just Keeps Coming At You

- His landlord threatened to kick him out of his apartment.
- He battles depression, as well as a fear of open spaces, and has to take 42 pills a day.

Despite everything, however, he hasn't given up. He still manages to have hope!

That's an imposing set of circumstances, isn't it? But his attitude is equally impressive. It reminds me of a passage in 1 Thessalonians 1:6 that talks about two opposites in life—affliction and joy, the hot water/cold water combination that spills out from our daily spigot. Gordon MacDonald says that only in Christ can these two things fit together comfortably in the same sentence, in the same verse, in the same life. Eugene Petersen, in *The Message*, translates the reference, "taking the trouble with the joy, the joy with the trouble." That's what we as God's people must learn to do.

In his book, *Searching for God Knows What*, Donald Miller discusses one of the causes for the afflictions we often face.

> I happened to see Larry King interview Billy Graham shortly after the shootings at Columbine High School

in Littleton, Colorado. I had read an article the previous month about violent video games and their effects on the minds of children. . . . Larry King asked Billy Graham what was wrong with the world and how such a thing as Columbine could happen. I knew, because Billy Graham was an educated man, he had read the same article I had read, and I began calculating his answer for him, that violence begets violence, that we live in a culture desensitized to the beauty of human life and the sanctity of creation. But Billy Graham did not blame video games.

Instead, Billy Graham referred back to the events that took place long, long ago—in the Garden of Eden.

Miller says what happened at that moment—man's decision to listen to Satan instead of God and the foothold the devil gained because of it—forever changed the course of our lives on this planet. It's the reason we have weeds in our vegetable gardens, and it's also the reason we have to deal with countless other difficult, challenging, and unpleasant things in life.

Matthew Bandy was a young 17-year-old who lied about his age so he could enlist in the Army. He ended up being one of the soldiers who parachuted onto the beach of Normandy on D-Day in 1944. Bandy had his instructions for what to do when he landed, but things didn't go as planned. A strong wind carried him away from the others and he ended up far off course. He could have been frightened, could have given up. But in an account written later, he said he made up his mind, "Wherever I landed, I was going to start the war from there!"

Sometimes, when life storms hit, our first reaction may be, "This wasn't supposed to happen!" Ever felt that way?

A friend of ours once preached a sermon entitled "The Journey of Life." He said, "On that journey, there ought to be a sign that says: *Watch for Falling Expectations.*" Disappointment is a main thoroughfare we all travel at one time or another.

Disappointment is a main thoroughfare we all travel at one time or another.

What should we do when things don't turn out like we'd hoped, when life just keeps coming at us? Let me tell you one more story from that trip we took to Montgomery. When we arrived, we were unloading our luggage. For some reason, we were determined to get it all inside by making just one trip. It was a real comedy act to anyone watching, I'm sure, as we struggled with so many bags that neither of us had a free hand to open the door. We had to put everything down, open it, then go through the long process of gathering it all back into our arms. The next day guess what we saw, just to the right of where we'd entered? An automatic door which we'd missed completely! How much easier it would have been to have used that instead of trying to do it all by ourselves.

So often in life, especially in the midst of storms, we fail to take advantage of the One who has said He'll help us. Instead, we stagger along, weighed down, trying to do it all on our own.

Paul Harvey tells the story of a little boy whose teacher asked what he did on his summer vacation. He replied he went to Minnesota to visit his grandma. "Wonderful!" the teacher replied. "Now, why don't you spell Minnesota for us?"

The little boy thought a moment. "Did I say Minnesota?" he said. "I meant Ohio. O-H-I-O!"

3 SURVIVING A TSUNAMI — *Life Just Keeps Coming At You*

FOR THOUGHT AND DISCUSSION

- Wouldn't it be great if life was always filled with what was easy and simple? Unfortunately, that's not the case. Yet it's from the hard and difficult—the Minnesota's—that we often learn the things we really need to know.

- What would life be like if everything was smooth and easy? You may think, "I'd like to find out!" More than likely, is that ever going to happen? Why or why not?

- Think of some people you really admire (this may be people you know or people you have heard of or read about). How have they been shaped by life that just keeps coming at them?

- Role play situations involving the following Bible characters and moments in their lives that didn't go exactly the way they expected.

- Mary, an unmarried pregnant teenager, telling her mom the news.

- Ruth, a young widow explaining to her parents that she's leaving town.

- David, on his deathbed, talking to Solomon about the temple he'd "intended" to build.

3 SURVIVING A TSUNAMI

Notes

Chapter 4

Trying times
are for trying.

The Lesson of Baby Giraffes

What role does God play in the storms of life? Is He the instigator—in other words, does He cause them? Or is He merely a spectator, One who sits back and watches as they hit?

I must admit when I contemplate the subject of this chapter, I can't help but be reminded of some answers a group of fifth graders gave once on a science test. The first question was, "What is a vibration?" One student wrote, "A vibration is a motion that can't make up its mind which way to go." That's me in a nutshell, trying to decide on a definitive explanation for God's part. Another question on the test was, "How are clouds formed?" A young boy answered, "I'm not sure. But clouds know how to do it and that's the important thing."

Let me assure you up front that I don't have all the answers on this topic. It's a rather involved matter. What we need to remember, though, above all else, is that God is in charge. He runs things and He knows what He's doing. That's what is important.

We've already talked in the previous chapter about the state of the world in which we live. Let me give you another good example, yet again courtesy of Donald Miller. Miller says, "I have on my desktop a picture of a boy named Sasha. Sasha is one of the children of Chernobyl, a young boy born after the disaster that happened when the core at a nuclear facility in Russia melted and leaked. This little boy, Sasha, is perhaps five years old, and he is gripping with a tiny arm the side of a crib. His other hand is flailing upward toward his ear, his head and shoulders the only portion of his body not mutated. On the right side of Sasha's chest rises a lump the size of a softball and his belly grows out disfigured before him as though he were pregnant, a truly painful sight. His legs are oversized and blocky and he has no knees, only rounded flesh flowing awkwardly to oversized feet, which produce four toes each, the largest of which, as big as my fist, is distanced from the others and pointing itself in an opposite direction. From the bottom of his stomach protrudes a rounded flow of flesh, as though it were a separate limb stopped in half growth. Sasha, the article in which I found the picture states, is in constant pain, lives in constant pain.

As terrible as it is to compare Sasha to ourselves, I have to go there. I have to say you and I were not supposed to be this way."

We were created to have a beautiful, wonderful relationship with our Maker, but then something happened which impacted not only us, but the world in which we live. We're scarred and incomplete, and the world around us—as well as the way it operates—is equally damaged.

The good news, though, is what God can accomplish despite this mess into which we've gotten ourselves. In John 9:1-7, we read about a man blind from birth. What a terrible life storm that was for him to endure, and not only him, but his parents as well. In verse two we see the principle of reciprocity which was so prevalent in those days—we also see it in the book of Job—where people thought suffering was a punishment for sin. Jesus explains to them that it doesn't work that way. My favorite part of the passage, however, is in verse 6. What did Jesus use to perform the miracle? He used mud—something made from dirt (yuck!) and spit (double yuck!). (It reminds me of when I was five and my cousin got the idea to mix dirt and water and tell everybody it was a new flavor of Kool-Aid.) Pretty disgusting, wouldn't you say? Yet—here's the beauty of it—God can take the mud in our lives and make a miracle out of it. He can take horrible things around us, horrible things that have happened, and use them to give us a clearer view of Him.

I once heard a preacher tell a story which I've never forgotten. His young daughter had been born with some type of medical problems (I forget the exact diagnosis). When she was very young, she had to be taken in to have a procedure done. His wife could not bring herself to watch, but the doctor asked him to stay in the room and help hold the child while they did whatever it was they had to do. The little girl wasn't old enough to talk, but her dad said he could imagine the thoughts she was having by the expression in her little eyes: "Daddy! Why are you letting this happen? Don't you know it hurts? Make it stop! I thought you loved me!"

That sounds so much like what we say to God at times, doesn't it?

It reminds me of a piece someone once shared with me entitled "Questions."

> *Lord, I ask more questions than You ask.*
> *The ratio, I would suppose, is ten to one.*
> *I ask—*
> *Why do You permit this anguish?*
> *How long can I endure?*
> *What possible purpose does it serve?*

Have You forgotten to be gracious?
Have I wearied You?
Have I offended You?
Have You cast me off?
Where did I miss Your guidance?
When did I lose my way?
Do you see my utter despair?
You ask:
Are you trusting Me?

In 1 Peter 1:3-9, we read how God very ingeniously uses Satan against himself. As He allows the devil to attack us, He uses those very attacks to bless us! The devil probably thinks, "Aha! I've got them now. I'll send this storm their way and they'll never recover." But God—if we'll let Him—can use that storm from Satan to make us even stronger.

In his book, ***A View from the Zoo***, Gary Richmond speaks of working at the Los Angeles Zoo. While there, he witnessed an Angola giraffe giving birth. "A calf, a plucky male, hurled forth, falling ten feet and landing on his back," he recalls. The mother giraffe, you see, gives birth from a standing position and the distance from the birth canal to the ground is about ten feet. (Yes, that's right – ten feet, about the height of a basketball goal!) Within a few seconds, the calf rolled to an upright position with his legs tucked under his body. What happened next, though, was totally unexpected. The mother giraffe lowered her head to look at the baby. Then, she swung her great long leg outward and kicked him so that he was sent sprawling! This happened not just once, but repeatedly. Every time the baby seemed to grow tired of trying to stand, the mother would give it another kick. And not only then—even when it at last managed to stand, it was kicked off its wobbly legs! Animal keeper Jack Badal explained to Richman the reason. It was, he said, because the mother wanted the calf to remember how it got up. In the wild, it would need to get up as quickly as possible to follow the herd. Lions, hyenas, leopards, and hunting dogs would devour it if it didn't.

When the storms of life knock us down, let's not let our souls shrivel with bitterness or despair, but instead grow bigger —spiritually— as a result.

What lesson is there in that for us? Am I saying that God kicks us around in life? Of course not. But I do believe He permits storms to come our way, storms which teach us lessons and make us stronger.

There's an interesting story told about Franklin D. Roosevelt. Before polio struck him in 1921, he was rather arrogant. But as he lay in bed recovering, he had a lot of time to reflect. His son James wrote of that period, "Lying there, he grew bigger." As his legs withered from the disease, his spirit broadened and deepened. He developed a deep compassion for others and went on in later life to become an advocate for those who were suffering.

May we be like Roosevelt. When the storms of life knock us down, let's not let our souls shrivel with bitterness or despair, but instead grow bigger—spiritually—as a result.

John Ortberg says, "Growth is what happens when you seek or exert control where you are able to rather than giving up in difficult circumstances. It happens when you decide to be wholly faithful in a situation you do not like and cannot understand."

FOR THOUGHT AND DISCUSSION

- Why are we more apt to grow from hard times than from times when everything goes smoothly?

- Think of examples where we as parents know something is good for our children or is something they need even though it may be unpleasant.

🌊 In what ways is our current world today totally different from the way God originally envisioned it?

🌊 What symbolism do you see in the fact that God uses "mud" to give us clearer vision?

🌊 The following is a situation in my life that I do not like and cannot understand:

🌊 This is how I will remain faithful and grow from it:

Notes

Chapter 5

"You can't unring a bell."

—*Dr. Phil*

There Are No Dogs

My husband and I are big soccer fans. We've been known to get up at unearthly hours and watch World Cup matches that are being played in countries on the other side of the world. For example, in the fall of 2007, we were able to watch part of a women's game between the United States and Brazil before going to work one morning. (We had a vested interest—not to mention divided loyalties—having lived in Brazil for six years in the 1980's.)

In that particular match, the North American women, who eventually lost 4-0, got down early on what is called an "own goal." One of their players, trying to clear out a ball, accidentally scored for the opponent. When that happened, the commentator said, "Now we'll see what these players are really made of. It's in the face of adversity—in other words, when somebody makes a mistake, when somebody gets hurt or goes down—that you find out just what kind of soccer team you have."

The same is true in life. It's not so hard to be a Christian when things are great, when everything is going our way. But when adversity comes along—when the ball bounces the wrong way and we find ourselves in a position we never expected or wanted—that's when we find out what kind of faith we really have. And that's when we have a choice. Will we quit? Will we give up? Will we decide it's just not worth it? Or will we take a deep breath, "suck it up" (as athletes say), and keep on playing?

In her book, *Ana's Story*, Jenna Bush tells the story of a 17-year-old girl in Panama who was born with HIV. At a group meeting for HIV victims, she changed people's perception by changing terminology, saying emphatically, "We are not dying with AIDS. We are living with it. We are survivors."

Surviving means learning to stick it out through the hard times, through life's storms. It isn't easy, but it is possible. However, one of the key steps in surviving is to realize you cannot make it on your own.

Notice another excerpt from Rick Von Feldt's first person account of the Asian tsunami:

> This was my fourth time to Phuket. During my years in Asia, I usually managed to get there for a business meeting or a long weekend holiday. One of the memories I had of Phuket were all the dogs. In many of the beach resorts, there were a lot of stray dogs. They ran around in packs. The Thai people have a friendliness to animals.

5 SURVIVING A TSUNAMI — *There Are No Dogs*

Each morning you could see packs of dogs playing down on the beach. They would run around chasing each other, playing doggy versions of tag. They would run along the beach road, looking for scraps of food or handouts from willing tourists.

But now there are no more dogs. {Washed up} with the bodies of people also come bodies of dogs.

On the morning of the wave, most were able to keep their heads above water when the first swell came. Dogs have a way of being able to swim. But when the second wave came, they were thrashed about and eventually dragged back into the ocean.

Let's notice some examples from the Bible of folks who were able to keep their heads above water not from their own strength, but with help from God.

One that comes to mind is Joseph. (Did you know that one-fourth of the book of Genesis is about him?) When we first meet him, Joseph's life was going along just fine. I imagine he thought everything was great. After all, he was his father's favorite son, and he had the coat to prove it! He was ensured of quite a future, too, evidenced by those recurring dreams of his. "Destined for greatness," as they say.

5 SURVIVING A TSUNAMI

Surely that had to be what the bowing sheaves and stars implied.

On the surface, Joseph appears a bit self-absorbed so I imagine he didn't have a clue as to how his brothers really felt about him. So what happened when they ganged up on him probably came as quite a shock. One minute his biggest problem was a detour from Shechem to Dothan and the next minute he was being mugged and dumped in a pit by those closest to him, his own family members! Talk about being hit by a tidal wave.

Joseph found meaning in a very simple way—by helping others.

And the story doesn't end there. We remember all the other layers of disappointment and despair that played out in his life. Fast forward a bit and we find him being stripped of his robe yet another time and having it used against him again. When Mrs. Potiphar dangled it before her husband and yelled, "Rape!" Joseph ended up in prison.

In prison, though, Joseph found meaning in a very simple way—by helping others. In particular he reached out to a couple of cell mates, a butler and a baker. It would have been so easy for him to have focused only on his own disappointment, only on the wrongs that had been done to him. (There were plenty of those!) That's what we often do. When life doesn't turn out the way we planned, we tend to forget that other people face disappointments too. We think only about ourselves.

Joseph, however, didn't do that. He saw beyond his own pain. Later on, after the butler had been restored to his position, he remembered Joseph. (It took a while, but he eventually remembered.)

Here's a question: What will people remember about your stay "in prison"—in other words, in the midst of a difficult situation? Will they remember that you fell apart, couldn't cope? Or will they remember that even in your pain and suffering, you reached out to others?

In prison, Joseph learned the inner workings of the Egyptian government, something which would prove invaluable to him in his later position. There are all kinds of things God will show us and teach us from our difficulties—if we are willing to learn.

A second example of one who survived an unexpected storm is David. Granted, he was the baby of the family and so he may have had a rough life from the beginning, putting up with ribbing from seven older brothers! But you have to admit after he got called in from the field to meet with Samuel, things went pretty well for a while.

Killed a giant. *Check*. Chosen as a special musician for the king. *Check*. Married to the king's daughter. *Check*. Inspiration for a popular song ("Saul has killed his thousands, but David his ten thousands"). *Check*. Suddenly, though, in one fatal swoop, everything was taken away by Saul's jealousy. Overnight David went from being a harp player to a sword dodger. The king who had treated him so royally turned on him, forcing David to leave everything (including his wife . . . who ended up being given to someone else!). He eventually was forced to hide in a cave.

At one point during his hiding—when a little makeshift village had been destroyed and family members of his ragtag band of followers taken captive—we're told that David and the people with him raised their voices and wept "until they had no more strength to weep." Have you ever cried like that, cried until there were no more tears inside you? Until you were so exhausted from weeping that you didn't have the energy to cry anymore?

In 1 Samuel 30:6—at one of the lowest points in David's life—we read, "But David found strength in the Lord his God" (NKJV). More than 40 times in the book of Psalms, he speaks of God being his refuge. "I'm hiding out under your wings," he writes, "until the hurricane blows over" (Psalm 57:1, *The Message*).

A third example is Job. Talk about someone having a bad day! Job, the most respected man in all of Uz (hey, even *God* had only good things to say about him!), lost everything in less than 24 hours. Everything—his camels, his donkeys, his oxen, his sheep, his servants, even his children. His children! How many parents have been driven to the brink of despair by the loss of one child, but Job in one day lost ten!

Then, instead of waking from his nightmare, it got worse. His body was plagued with boils and his supposed helpmeet—doubtless stunned by overwhelming grief herself—instead of offering words of comfort and solace, told him just to curse God and die.

There are several lessons to be learned from Job. First of all, no one ever has all the facts in a situation involving suffering. Job concluded that he was righteous and God was being unfair. His friends insisted on the opposite: that God was righteous and Job was being rightfully punished. We know that all of them were viewing the situation from a limited perspective, blind to the real struggle being waged not even on the planet, but rather in heaven between God and Satan!

Another thing to consider is that Job could have lost his sanity playing the "What If?" game. Job 1:4 tells us that his sons had invited their three sisters to eat and drink with them. Afterwards, Job probably thought to himself, "If only I hadn't let my daughters go to the feast that day! What if I'd made them stay home? Or why didn't I just tell all my sons to come over here?"

When bad things happen, the tendency is to go over and over certain events and think, "If only I'd done this" or "If only I hadn't done that."

Focus on the Family founder Dr. James Dobson says the first principle of mental health is to accept that which cannot be changed. In other words, recognize that what has happened has happened. Much as you might like to, you can't go back and undo it. You have to accept and learn to deal with what has taken place. Job did that.

Something else I read about Job was fascinating. Do you remember what happened at the end of the story? Everything Job had was restored to him double. Once owner of seven thousand sheep, three thousand camels, five hundred yoke of oxen and five hundred donkeys, he was given fourteen thousand sheep, six thousand camels, one thousand yoke of oxen, and one thousand donkeys. Significantly, though, his family did not double. The father of seven sons and three daughters became father of seven new sons and three new daughters—not fourteen sons and six daughters. Why was that? Many Bible scholars take this as a reassurance to Job that one day he will get his original family back. The ten children he lost so tragically will be restored to him. That's a beautiful thought, and one to which the book of Revelation gives credence. God will right all the wrongs from the storms we face!

FOR THOUGHT AND DISCUSSION

- How does focusing on others help you get through your own personal storms?

- Why is it important to be able to accept what has happened? Do you have to be able to understand something before you can accept it? Why or why not?

5 SURVIVING A TSUNAMI — *There Are No Dogs*

🌊 During his storm, Joseph learned things that would be invaluable to him later in life. Think of a lesson you've learned from your storms.

🌊 Have you ever tried to dog paddle your own way out of a rough situation? Why is this not effective in a major crisis?

Notes

Chapter 6

"Everything that was not tied down was sucked back with {the waves}."

—*Rick Von Feldt*

Below the Waterline

During the years our family lived in Brazil, we did our best to celebrate American holidays, even those which weren't recognized overseas. Thanksgiving was probably the easiest—we were with a team of other Americans so it was simply a matter of gathering at someone's house for a big meal (minus the football, of course). Halloween proved a bit more of a challenge. We took our kids trick-or-treating to one another's homes, but costumes were always interesting since there was nothing available to buy in stores. The last year we were there, the Halloween horror movies had come out in theatres, so Brazilians knew about the tradition from those. We decided it might be fun to host a party for the teenagers at church and have everybody dress up. I got the idea to make the six of us—me, my husband and our four children—matching skeleton costumes. I bought some black fabric and got a friend who was very artistic to paint the bones. We looked cute, if I do say so myself! The only problem was I was a cheapskate. For some reason (probably because I knew they wouldn't be worn a lot), I scrimped and bought very inexpensive fabric. The night of the party, our kids—ages one, three, five and seven—were running around, jumping up and down, doing all the things that kids that age do, and their costumes fell apart. They literally ripped at the seams!

When hard times in life hit, some people come unraveled. What keeps us from falling apart at the seams?

The key, of course, is how well we're put together beforehand. What quality is the fabric of our lives, specifically when it comes to spiritual matters? The stronger it is, the better chance we have of enduring.

I don't know a lot about boats, never having been much of a water person. But I have read that sailboats, for the most part, don't ever capsize. They are built to take the most vigorous pounding the sea can dish out and still stay afloat. Of all sailing vessels, a sailboat is the one most likely to be able to right itself were the wind to push it over or turn it upside down. Do you know why? The answer is very simple. It is because it has more weight below the waterline than it does above it.

Remember the story of the wise man and foolish man in Matthew 7? It all gets back to a matter of foundation. How well are you grounded?

Unfortunately, in today's world, much of our emphasis is on superficial things—that which is above ground. A poet once wrote:

> *Life is mostly froth and bubbles*
> *Two things stand out like stone*
> *Kindness in another's troubles*
> *Courage in your own.*

Webster defines froth as something "insubstantial, trivial."

A missionary I know often said, "If you're coming to see my house, give me a week to get it ready. But if you're coming to see me, you can come anytime." Relationships have much more value than physical things and possessions and therefore deserve greater emphasis. Yet we often forget that.

Our world is full of froth and bubbles. The first Bible class I ever taught after becoming a Christian was cradle roll. To a 13-year-old, a room full of babies can be pretty scary. But I knew that there was one thing I could fall back on. When the story was told and I'd sung—by myself, of course—every song I'd ever known, I could always blow bubbles! Babies loved them. And who wouldn't? They were light and pretty and floated all around. When you think about it, though, they're also empty and meaningless and gone in the snap of a finger. So is life.

Back in 1960, an eight-year-old boy named Walter Sedor was found, hungry and afraid, sitting on a rock less than a mile from Tarton Lake near Flin Flon, Manitoba. He and his father had been on a fishing trip. For 15 days, Walter had waited beside the remains of the small aircraft which had crashed, killing his father Steve. Royal Canadian Air Force and civilian planes scanned 70,000 square miles of land for days before finding Walter waving feebly for help. He had been without food and water for more than two weeks and was very close to starving. The sad thing was there was no need for this to have happened because in the wreckage of the plane, there was a survival kit containing 24 days' ration of food. But the boy didn't know it was there.

We're lost and starving and suffering when right beside us the whole time is a survival kit unopened and unused.

Many times we're like Walter. We're lost and starving and suffering when right beside us the whole time is a survival kit unopened and unused. God's Word, the Bible, contains the daily rations we need, everything to get us through life's crashes and crises.

You may have seen the following discussion of the difference between a fern and a bamboo plant.

> One day I decided to quit. I quit my job, my relationship, my spirituality. I wanted to quit my life. I went to the woods to have one last talk with God.
>
> "God," I said. "Can you give me one good reason not to quit?"
>
> His answer surprised me. "Look around," He said. "Do you see the fern and the bamboo?"
>
> "Yes," I replied.
>
> "When I planted the fern and the bamboo seeds, I took very good care of them. I gave them light. I gave them water. The fern quickly grew from the earth. Its brilliant green covered the floor. Yet nothing came from the bamboo seed. But I did not quit on the bamboo. In the second year the fern grew more vibrant and plentiful. And again, nothing came from the bamboo seed. But I did

not quit on the bamboo. In year three, there still was nothing from the bamboo seed. But I would not quit. In year four, again there was nothing from the bamboo seed. I would not quit. Then in the fifth year, a tiny sprout emerged from the earth. Compared to the fern, it was seemingly small and insignificant. But just six months later the bamboo rose to over 100 feet tall! It had spent five years growing roots. Those roots made it strong and gave it what it needed to survive. I would not give any of My creations a challenge it could not handle."

He said to me, "Did you know, my child, that all this time you have been struggling, you have actually been growing roots? I would not quit on the bamboo. I will never quit on you.

Don't compare yourself to others. The bamboo had a different purpose than the fern. Yet they both make the forest beautiful. Your time will come."

God said to me, "You will rise high."

"How high should I rise?" I asked.

"How high will the bamboo rise?" He asked in return.

"As high as it can?" I questioned.

"Yes," He said. "Give Me glory by rising as high as you can."

I remember when our children were young, they had some blowup toys that were weighted in the bottom. They made delightful punching bags because no matter how hard you knocked them or how many times they were slung to the ground, they always bounced right back to an upright position. With the proper foundation—spiritual weight below the waterline—we too can be resilient.

FOR THOUGHT AND DISCUSSION

- If you want to make something that will last, how do you make it? What kind of materials are used? What type of construction is employed?

- Could much of our life here on earth be categorized as "froth and bubbles"? Why or why not?

- Is most of your daily emphasis on things above or below the waterline? Should this be changed or altered? How?

- Discuss the Christian's emphasis on things "not seen."

- Why do people go into cellars and basements during storms? Why is there safety below the surface?

- The New Testament talks about going into an "inner closet" for prayer. What figurative security can this give one from life storms?

Notes

Chapter 7

"The more complicated
the actual conditions are,
the more delightfully
joyful it is to see
God open up
His way through."

—*Oswald Chambers*

Seeing the Shore

In 1952 Florence Chadwick attempted to swim the cold ocean seas between Catalina Island and the California shore. For 15 hours, she swam in foggy weather through the choppy water. As her muscles began to cramp, she lost some of her resolve and begged to be picked up. However her mother, who was riding in a boat alongside her, urged her to keep going. She tried her best, but finally grew too exhausted to continue. Aides lifted her out of water up into the boat. In just a few short minutes, the mist broke at last. When that happened, Chadwick saw that the shore was less than half a mile away. "All I could see was the fog," she explained later at a news conference. "I think if I could have seen the shore, I would have made it."

We must learn to look through the fog of whatever storm threatens to overtake our lives. We may be closer to the end of it than we think.

Someone has said that the biggest party in hell was held on the Saturday night before Christ's resurrection. At the time, Satan thought he had won, thought he had managed to kill the Son of God. As the old saying goes, things truly can be darkest right before the dawn.

What if Naaman had given up after dipping only six times in the River Jordan (2 Kings 5)?

What if the Israelites had gotten discouraged on their fifth day of marching around the city of Jericho (Joshua 6)?

What if Noah had given up on in the 119th year of preaching as he was readying an ark for the flood (Genesis 7)?

According to an old fable, a boy lived with his father at the base of a large dam. Every day the father would go to work on the mountain behind their house and return home with a wheelbarrow full of dirt. "Pour the dirt in the sacks, son," the father would say. "And stack them in front of the house."

And though the boy would obey, he also complained. He was tired of dirt. He was weary of bags. Why didn't his father give him what other fathers gave their sons? They had toys and games; he had dirt. When he saw what the others had, he grew mad at them. "It's not fair," he said to himself.

And when he saw his father, he objected. "They have fun. I have dirt."

The father would smile and place his arm on the boy's shoulders and say, "Trust me, son. I'm doing what is best."

But it was so hard for the boy to trust. Every day the father would bring the load. Every day the boy would fill the bags. "Stack them as high as you can," the father would say as he went for more. And so the boy filled the bags and piled them high. So high he couldn't see over them.

"Work hard, son," the father said one day. "We're running out of time." As the father spoke, he looked at the darkening sky. The boy stared at the clouds and turned to ask about them, but when he did, the thunder cracked and the sky opened. The rain poured so hard he could scarcely see his father through the water. "Keep stacking, son!" And as he did, the boy heard a mighty crash.

The water of the river poured through the dam and toward the little village. In a moment the tide swept everything in its path, but the dike of dirt gave the boy and the father the time they needed. "Hurry, son. Follow me."

They ran to the side of the mountain behind their house and into a tunnel. In a matter of moments they exited the other side and scampered up the hill and came upon a new cottage.

"We'll be safe here," the father said to the boy.

Only then did the son realize what the father had done. He had burrowed an exit. Rather than give him what he wanted, the father gave his boy what he needed. He gave him a safe passage and a safe place.

My cousin and her husband recently lost their 22-year-old son, their only child, in a car accident. As is always the case when a young person dies, it was such a tragedy. But I have been so impressed with the attitude they have exhibited throughout this storm. They determined that the funeral service was to be a celebration of Jarrod's life. They even walked in to the hymn "Sing and Be Happy." (In this, they reminded me of the people of Jehoshaphat's day. In 2 Chronicles 20, we read that the king, having been assured of victory, placed singers at the front of his army to lead them into battle. In Christ, we too can face our enemies—even that greatest enemy, death—with a song on our lips!)

> *Sing and be happy.*

One of the speakers at the memorial service was the principal at the elementary school Jarrod had attended. He remembered that as a five-year-old, Jarrod wasn't very happy about having to start school. In fact, he cried every day the first two weeks. His mom, after trying everything she could think of, finally suggested that the principal promise Jarrod a sucker at the end of the school day if he wouldn't cry. It worked like a charm! So the principal kept a drawer full of suckers in his desk, and that got them through the crisis. The promise of what was to come made those long hours away from Mom bearable. The principal also told how Jarrod grew up to be a terrific soccer player, so good that his senior year, he was offered a scholarship to an out-of-state college. He went, but due to being homesick, only stayed a few weeks. Apparently, the principal said, they didn't have any suckers there!

God's promise of what awaits us at the end of time should be enough to get us through our long day here on earth.

In 2 Corinthians 4:17, we read, "For our light and momentary troubles are achieving for us an eternal glory that far outweighs them all" (NKJV).

"Light" and "momentary" may not be words that you would choose to describe a particular storm you are facing. But we must remember that in comparison to eternity, any time here on earth is just a blimp on the radar.

In Valladolid, Spain, where Christopher Columbus died in 1506, there is a statue commemorating the man who discovered the New World. The memorial contains a figure of Columbus and a figure of a lion. At the bottom is engraved a Latin phrase, the Spanish National Motto.

Their motto—selected before Columbus' voyage—was "No More Beyond." At that point in time, you see, they honestly believed they had reached the outer limits of earth. His discovery, however, proved that was not the case.

On the memorial, therefore, the lion has his paw extended and covers up the first word of the phrase. All that is visible are the two words meaning "More Beyond."

What a beautiful reminder this story is for the Christian! In our darkest storms, we need to remember that there is more—much, much more—beyond our life here on this earth.

FOR THOUGHT AND DISCUSSION

- Why is it important for us to "look through the fog"?
- Read James 4:14. How long does fog usually last?
- How are we like the people of Spain in pre-Columbus days? Do we live as though we believe there is "No More Beyond" this present life?
- What has God promised us at the end of life's long day? Describe what will make it so special.

Notes

Chapter 8

"Many still hear the thundering in their heads."

—from newspaper accounts of the tsunami

God With Us in the Fire

Gordon MacDonald, in his book *The Life God Blesses*, says that one of his greatest memories of being a father was putting his children to bed at night.

> After evening prayers, I would kiss our little girl and head for the door. There the bedtime liturgy was no less important. The door was to be shut within six inches so that the hall light could cast a glow into the room . . . but not directly. And as I would slip out the door, there would be this final exchange – almost always word for word:
>
> "Where will you be, Daddy?"
>
> "I'll be in the living room with Mom, sweetheart."
>
> "Do you think you'll stay there till I go to sleep?"
>
> "No doubt about it. You can call me if you need me."
>
> "OK. But now, don't go to sleep until I'm asleep."
>
> "Don't you worry. I love you, honey. Good night."

"I love you, too, Daddy. Good night."

Where will you be? That is no small question for a child seeking the reassurance that her father or mother will be within shouting distance; no small question either for one who seeks after the God who has said that He desires to inhabit the soul and that He will always be near.

Where will you be, God?

Throughout the Bible, time and time again, we see God, our loving Father, reassuring His children with the words: "I will be with you."

Nowhere in Scripture is this more evident than in the story of Hananiah, Mishael, and Azariah. What's that? You don't recall such a story? Okay, so perhaps they're better known as Shadrach, Meshach, and Abednego. (Or, as one child called them, "Your Shack, My Shack, and To Bed You Go"!)

The Biblical story of the fiery furnace has long been a Sunday school favorite. In fact, it's probably one of the best known miracles in either the Old or New Testaments. (The greatest

> *Throughout the Bible, time and time again, we see God, our loving Father, reassuring His children with the words: "I will be with you."*

miracle, one little boy said, was when Joshua told his son to stand still and he did!)

In 1844 James Knox Polk was elected President of the United States. Polk was a very unassuming figure—only five foot six inches in height—and rather quiet at times. It bothered his wife Sarah that when he walked into a room of dignitaries, even at the White House, he often went unnoticed. So she requested the selection of a song to be played, announcing his presence, each time he entered a room. Someone chose what we now call *"Hail to the Chief,"* originally a boat song composed in 1828 by James Sanderson.

"Hail to the Chief" wasn't available in the days of Nebuchadnezzar, king of Babylon, but he still got his due. Musical instruments of that era called people to bow down and worship a big 90-foot statue he erected.

This image, which scholars tell us could probably be seen fifteen miles in any direction on the plains of Mesopotamia, was probably overlaid with gold and not solid through and through. But, as one commentator says, the faith of God's servants in the events that followed, proved to be purer gold than the actual statue itself!

Daniel 3 tells us that Shadrach, Meshach, and Abednego refused to bow down to the statue. In verse 15, Nebuchadnezzar basically gives them a second chance, thinking perhaps their refusal was the result of misunderstanding the rules (after all, they were foreigners). But their reply in verse 16 shows their minds were already made up. This angered the king and he ordered the fire made hotter. (Ever notice that anger usually expresses itself with superlatives? Did your children ever say, "You're the MEANEST mother in the world?")

You're familiar with the way the story plays out—the three Hebrews were thrown into the fiery furnace and a miracle occurred, involving seven facets:

1) They survived. They weren't killed instantly like the men who threw them in.

2) They walked around loosed, when they had fallen in bound.

3) There was a fourth man in the fire with them.

4) The fire did not alter their bodies in any way whatsoever.

5) Their hair was not even singed.

6) Their clothing remained intact.

7) There was not even the smell of fire on them.

From this story, there are several lessons we can learn.

First, God turned the blaspheming of His name into a praise of His name. (See Daniel 3:28,29.)

Secondly, the actions of the Hebrew children were a tremendous testimony. When they spoke of their God at the beginning of the incident, no one believed. But when they supported the truth of His existence by putting their trust in Him in the face of great trial, then people believed. Today people will come much nearer believing if they see us trusting God through our trials of fire rather than just talking about Him. Storms present a great opportunity for influencing and reaching others.

Third, the attitude of Shadrach, Meshach, and Abednego was worthy of imitation. Whatever God did, they said, was up to Him. They accepted in advance the outcome.

A woman was aboard a European luxury liner during a terrible storm. Everyone else panicked, but this lady gathered all the young children together and began telling Bible stories to keep them calm. Fortunately, the ship made it through safely. Later the captain was walking by and asked this woman how she kept so calm. "Have you been through something like this before?"

"No," the woman replied. "But you see I have two daughters. One of them lives in New York. I'm on my way to visit her. The other one passed away as a child. She lives in heaven. So I knew no matter what happened, either way I would be seeing one of my daughters in a few hours. And it really didn't make any difference to me which one it was."

Fourthly, God was with them. Often in basketball games, coaches have a designated "sixth man," someone whose role is coming in off the bench and providing a much-needed spark. Well, in this story a "fourth man" came in and prevented a spark!

Who was it? Nebuchadnezzar first said "a Son of God," then referred to him as an angel. Many scholars believe it was God Himself.

The bottom line is in our worst moments, when things look their bleakest, when we're not even sure we're going to make it, God is there beside us! All is not lost when we think it is.

Even though we can't see Him, we can be assured that God is with us during the storms of our lives. He knows what we're going through, and, more than just that, He goes through it with us!

In Matthew 10:30, we're told that God even knows the number of hairs on our heads! That's a very special verse for women because what do we obsess over any more than our hair? Half the time our husbands don't even notice when we get our hair cut, but God knows the exact number of hard-to-manage strands on our noggin! That's a very intimate knowledge.

> *He that keepeth thee will not slumber. Behold, He that keepeth Israel shall neither slumber nor sleep.*
>
> *— Psalm 121:3,4*

I read once that this thought is very comforting to women cancer patients who must undergo chemotherapy. Most of the time hair loss is inevitable with such treatments. That's one of the great traumas of cancer for females. One woman wrote, "It helped when I looked in the mirror every day to remember that God knew the number of hairs on my head. I was glad someone was keeping inventory! I numbered those hairs myself sadly, watching them fall out. But He knew the exact total."

He knows everything about us. And if He numbers the hairs on your head, don't you think He's up to date on the larger issues in your life as well?

An old preacher worked into the early morning hours trying to solve various problems. It just so happened that the Bible on his desk was open to Psalm 121. At a moment of intense exhaustion, his eyes fell on the startling words in that passage (verses 3 and 4) that told him God never sleeps.

He said it was almost as if the Lord were saying, "My child, there's no need for both of us to stay up all night. I'm going to be up anyway. You go on to bed and get a good night's sleep."

Alexander the Great once said that he never lost any sleep. He was asked how that could be when he was constantly surrounded by danger. He replied that Parmenio, his faithful guard, kept watch so he could rest.

If a general could sleep with a mere man watching over him, how much more should we be able to rest knowing God is watching over us? His care is constant. He is with us. What reassurance!

> *He will not suffer thy foot to be moved: he that keepeth thee will not slumber.*
>
> *Behold, he that keepeth Israel shall neither slumber nor sleep.* —*Psalm 121:3,4*

FOR THOUGHT AND DISCUSSION

- Do most people have a fear of being alone? Why is that?

- Why are difficult things easier to handle if you have someone beside you?

- What does it say about our God in that He not only rescued Shadrach, Meshach, and Abednego, but was with them as they experienced the fiery furnace?

- How can Jesus better relate to us because of the things He experienced on earth as a man?

- Describe the way our situation compares to the woman on the luxury liner.

Chapter 9

"Although the world is full of sorrow, it is also full of the overcoming of it."

—Helen Keller

No Pat Formulas

A popular author talked recently about his struggle with smokeless tobacco. In a valiant effort to kick the habit, he went to web sites and looked up the statistics about the health risks involved. He even printed them out to look at when he was tempted. But that didn't do any good; he still purchased the product, still used it. Then one day on the radio he heard a public service message about the danger of chewing tobacco. The man speaking said he'd had half his jaw removed and that he had no lower lip, all because of cancer. That did it. "I never used the stuff again," the author says.

Sometimes what really touches us or speaks to our hearts, what helps the most has nothing to do with an intellectual, step-by-step process. It's much more personal. That's why there are no cut-and-dried, sure-fire formulas for surviving a storm. Others may try to offer them, but what works for one person doesn't automatically guarantee success for another.

A newspaper article from *USA Today* in September of 2005 is interesting. In the aftermath of Hurricane Katrina, reporters interviewed veterans of other natural disasters—such as floods, tornadoes, and earthquakes. They asked these people to share what they had learned from their experiences and give advice to the victims of Katrina.

We've noted already the similarities between literal furies of nature which shake, uproot, and destroy, and those figurative storms which wreak a different kind of havoc but nevertheless can turn personal worlds upside down. The advice given by survivors of both is similar as well. For example:

• *Go slow and have faith.* Initially you think, "There's no way I'm going to get out of this," but you will.

• *Lean on others.* The biggest thing is being able to rely on a close network of friends and family.

• *Be patient.* It will probably take longer to recover than you think.

Back in March of 1996 the late actor Christopher Reeve, paralyzed from a riding accident, got a standing ovation when he appeared on stage at the Oscars. "What you may not know," he joked to the crowd, "is that I left New York in September to get here on time!" He was being funny, but, fact of the matter is, storms take time to get over. It's a slow journey.

After Hurricane Ivan in 2004, officials in Pensacola said, "The rebuilding will take years." That's just as true after emotional storms as it is after physical ones.

Trouble is, of course, when you're in the midst of a storm, time seems to stand still. You want to fast forward one year or two or five to where it doesn't hurt so much, but you can't. You have to concentrate on small increments of time—getting through one day, for example.

In the November 2007 issue of ***Christian Chronicle***, Emily Lemley discussed the effects of a storm which hit her family in the mid-1970's. Her father, minister at a large church in Texas, was involved in an alcohol-related automobile crash. Her comments concerning how their family survived that incident are worth sharing, I believe, because many storms in life are high profile and cause public embarrassment.

The first thing she mentioned was negative. She said at the time of the accident, she had two small children, whom she felt were too young to understand what was happening. So she chose not to tell them, intending to wait until they were a little older. However, before she could do it at her chosen time, the children heard about it from someone at church. What a shame.

In the movie *Twister*, individuals known as storm chasers followed the trail of tornadoes just for the thrill of it. Sometimes, if we're not careful, we may have the tendency to do the same thing with figurative storms! We thrive on scandal and enjoy dishing about the latest trauma in someone else's life. *Have you heard about so-and-so?* But guess what? It's a little different when it's our own life being examined under the microscope. A worthy motto is always, "Pray more than you say." Let's go to God on behalf of people who are experiencing storms in their lives rather than gossiping about them.

Another comment Emily Lemley made focused on the positive. She said that God forgave her father and—eventually—the church reflected that forgiveness. We don't ever seem to forgive as readily and as quickly as our Father, do we? We're much better at remembering past wrongs and holding grudges.

> *A worthy motto is always, "Pray more than you say."*

Emily also said that the years after the accident were her father's "most authentic." Storms can purify and help us better focus on our purpose. In his later years, her dad was able to reach out in a very special way to others dealing with addiction.

Something survivors need to be willing to consider is getting help from outside sources, whether it be counseling or medication. As Christians, sometimes we are hesitant to do this, thinking that our faith should be able to take care of all our problems. Many times people taking something for depression even say, "If I were a stronger Christian, I could overcome this on my own." It is never a sign of weakness to want help; in fact, it is a sign of strength to be willing to accept it.

An article from the September 2007 *Gospel Advocate* says:

> The medicines we have available all come from things the Lord created. Pharmaceutical companies have specialists who roam remote parts of the world looking for sources of healing that have long been known by the natives. One should just as readily accept medical help for depression as he or she accepts aspirin for a headache.

Another suggestion involves using journaling to ease the trauma of a life storm.

"People who write for twenty minutes a day about traumatic events reduce their doctor visits, improve their immune systems and, among arthritis sufferers, use less medication and have greater mobility," says James W. Pennebaker, Ph.D., a professor at the University of Texas, who has conducted studies on the topic. Writing about the event causing anxiety can help organize the experience and eventually help individuals move past it.

Singer Judy Collins found writing about her experiences helpful after her son and only child, Clark Taylor, committed suicide in 1992. In describing that ordeal, she says, "I was beyond devastation. I wanted to die, to pack it in, call it a day, call it quits, stop in my tracks . . . . Now he was gone. I could not see a way to live beyond that terrible day."

Coming out of what she calls "the shock of the horrible loss, you think everything is over . . . and you'll never have a happy life." But writing about the tragedy and talking to others helped her cope.

Seeking out the stories of survivors, if nothing else, can give you reassurance that others have made it through bleak periods, and you will as well. Their guides, while not a step-by-step process you can duplicate, can nevertheless be comforting.

FOR THOUGHT AND DISCUSSION

- Why do you think we long for methodical, step-by-step solutions to our challenges in life?

- What things in life—other than storms—can't be explained or dealt with in simple "how to" instructions?

- Why are we so fascinated by storms in the lives of others?

- Do we ever try to salve our consciences about our own situations in comparison?

- Is taking medication for an emotional problem any different than taking it for a physical problem? Why or why not?

Chapter 10

"We all got a little junk in the trunk . . ."

—*"Don't Worry 'Bout A Thing"*
SHeDAISY

The Cycle of Comfort

If anybody ever sounded like a broken record, it might be the Apostle Paul in the first chapter of 2 Corinthians. Five times in one sentence (verses 3 and 4), he talks about the same idea—comfort.

What is comfort? Webster's says it means "to give hope and strength; to quiet grief and trouble; to cheer."

My daughter has a friend who recently broke up with her boyfriend. Several in the girl's closest group of friends went together and sent her a bouquet of flowers. Why? For comfort. But who is the best comforter of all, even better than girlfriends who show up, bring chocolate and sad movies, and cry with you over a heartbreak? God! The Bible says He is the God of all comfort. It reminds me of that phrase "mother of all wars." God is the epitome of comfort; there is none above Him. 2 Thessalonians 2:16 says He gives us "eternal comfort" (NIV). According to the passage in 2 Corinthians, though, there's a reason He does this. Obviously, He cares about us, but beyond that, as verse 4 says, He comforts us so that we, in turn, can comfort others.

The Message puts it this way:

> All praise to the God and Father of our Master, Jesus the Messiah! Father of all mercy! God of all healing counsel! He comes alongside us when we go through hard times, and before you know it, he brings us alongside someone else who is going through hard times so that we can be there for that person just as God was there for us.

God, you see, can empower us by using the misfortune in our lives to make us better comforters. As the song says, "Sometimes we laugh together, sometimes we cry." Romans 12:15 reminds us that we are to be with our fellow Christians both in times of joy and times of sorrow.

Yet, our tendency is to go about our day-to-day life focusing only on things that affect us personally. Often those things are superficial. When adversity strikes, however, it changes our focus and makes us look at what is of lasting importance. Then, we realize how much we need others!

We're like the little girl who was crying in her room after going to bed. When her mom went to check on her, the child explained that she was afraid of the dark. "Honey," her mom said, "there's no need to be afraid. Remember, God is with you."

"I know," the little girl replied with a sniffle. "But I need someone in here with skin on!"

Surely nothing gives us greater comfort than having at our side a physical presence to remind us that we are not facing our difficulty alone.

> ***The best comforter is one who has struggled with personal pain and sorrow and emerged victorious.***

The best comforter is one who has struggled with personal pain and sorrow and emerged victorious.

In a July 2007 publication from *Focus on the Family*, Dee Brestin (who lost her 59-year-old husband to cancer) writes:

> I don't particularly enjoy being around Christians who haven't suffered deeply. They can be like Job's friends, offering pat answers, misapplying God's truths. They smile and quote Scriptures to me. I cringe.

They send a card with a platitude pointing out the silver lining to my pain. I close it quickly. I *know* they mean well.

But, oh, the comfort of being with those who have suffered! They've been there, so they know better than to tell me God is sovereign and all things work together for our good. I *know* that's true, but I can't hear it now.

High-tide grief is not the time to speak solutions. (Women who have had miscarriages tell me the last thing they want to hear is, "You can have another baby.") When one is grieving, it is the time for friends to be silent, to hug, and to weep.

I don't know why it diminishes grief to have someone weep with you, but it does. Friends who cry with me are like Ruth, who, having lost her own husband, could stand beside Naomi without trying to fix the unfixable.

True friends understand that there is no instant cure to make pain go away. Job's friends were most effective in the first seven days when they sat with him and said nothing at all. Have you ever thought about how much shorter the book would be without all their attempts at explanation and advice?

Once during Queen Victoria's reign, she heard that the wife of a common laborer had lost her baby. Having experienced deep sorrow herself, she felt moved to express her sympathy. So one day she called on the bereaved woman and spent some time with her. After she'd left, the neighbors were curious as to what the queen had said. "Nothing at all," replied the grieving mother. "She simply put her hands on mine, and we silently wept together."

Of course what is comforting to a person may vary, depending upon the situation. A woman who experienced problems with her teenage son says she appreciated those who, instead of treating her with pity, acted as though nothing had happened. "When I was in the throes of pain, just a normal conversation with someone meant the world to me," she explains.

This same idea is evident in a conversation between two women on a recent television program. One of them asks the other if she and her husband are having financial problems. "It's okay if you are," she says.

"Is that so?" replies the second woman.

"Yes, and to tell you the truth, I'm a little insulted.

I am a good friend. Why would you feel like you have to hide that from me?"

"I don't know," the second woman replies, adding that perhaps it's for the same reason that her friend hasn't shared with her the marital problems she is experiencing.

"That," her friend replies stiffly, "is obviously different."

"Why? Because it happened to you? This is how I see it. Good friends support each other after they've been humiliated. Great friends pretend nothing happened in the first place."

Obviously ignoring a problem isn't going to make it go away. And while we may not want—or need—to bear our souls to everyone that comes along, it can be good therapy to have at least one good friend in whom to confide.

One of the best known passages of comfort in the New Testament is John 14:1-3. It is the remedy for troubled hearts, prescribed by the Great Physician Himself. Interesting enough, Jesus spoke these words right after He told that Peter would deny Him. He knew Peter would fail and He knew how devastated he would be by it. Jesus knows everyone's failures—our own and the failures of those we love. But in those bleak moments of despair, when a storm has swept in and we feel like our lives are over, His Words provide comfort. "Others may let you down," He seems to be saying. "You may let yourself down. But I won't let you down. If it were not so, I would have told you."

Real comfort equips one to patiently endure. Most people tend to think they can only be comforted if they feel better or if circumstances change. The Bible teaches that we can be hopeful because we know God will sustain us (2 Corinthians 12:9).

FOR THOUGHT AND DISCUSSION

- Think of a time in life when someone comforted you. How did they do it?

- Discuss the television character's description of a great friend. Do you agree? Why or why not?

- Why do children run to a parent when they are hurt? What are they seeking?

- Discuss the idea of "comfort food." What is meant by that expression? How can something we eat console us?

- How does God "train" us to be comforters by giving us comfort Himself in our hard times?

- List specific ways you can comfort those going through the storms below:

    — death of a loved one
    — chronic illness
    — divorce or marital struggles
    — caring for elderly parents
    — problems with children
    — financial uncertainties

Notes

Chapter 11

"God rarely forces Himself upon us, but He prepares a loaded tray of help and sets it right outside the door. We have to open the door to retrieve it."

—*Susan Owings*

How You Finish

In Jeremiah 20:18, the prophet asks, *Why was I ever born? My entire life has been filled with trouble, sorrow, and shame.* We all may have moments when we feel like that. When you're in the middle of a storm, especially, it's hard to see past the pain.

One of my favorite videos of all I've seen on the Internet is a little girl—probably three or four years old—quoting Psalm 23. It is so cute! She starts out really strong and confident, but after the first couple of verses she slows down a bit and is obviously a little confused about what comes next. She turns to someone off camera and it sounds like she's saying, "Shirley? Shirley?" I couldn't figure it out at first because her dad is filming her (you can hear him in the background). Finally, it dawned on me that she wasn't saying the woman's name "Shirley," but was asking if it was time for the line "Surely goodness and mercy will follow me."

> *Why was I ever born? My entire life has been filled with trouble, sorrow, and shame.*

Her dad prompts her with the next key word, and she quotes a little more and then pauses again and asks, "Shirley? Shirley?"

One of my friends says this reminds her so much of the way we are with our Father, questioning Him about the same line. "Surely goodness and mercy will follow us, Lord? Didn't you promise that? Well, this storm I'm facing is not good. Where is Your mercy in this situation? SURELY You didn't mean for this to happen to me, did You?"

From Job, we learn that it's not unusual or wrong to have questions when the hard times come. That's normal. What we need to do, though, even when we don't understand what's happening, is remember that God is in control. He can be trusted to bring us through whatever it is we're facing.

And guess what? Eventually the storms will subside.

I got an email recently from a college friend who currently lives in Panama. She and her husband have retired from teaching and are doing mission work. She asked what I was doing, and I replied that I was writing a book on the storms of life. "Any words of wisdom to share?" I asked.

"How many chapters do you want?" she responded, and I could imagine her smiling as she wrote.

"I could write volumes on surviving the storms of raising an adopted, ADD, emotionally-charged and issue-filled child," she went on to say. "When our son joined the Navy at 18 and left home, we actually said it was like a storm had passed. I think we were shell-shocked for months before we finally relaxed and realized it was really over."

If you—like my friend—can look back on a storm in life that has finally subsided, you know there's a lot for which to be thankful. You also know you're a stronger person having weathered that particular storm.

I won't ever forget my first pregnancy. To say I was nervous about childbirth would be an understatement. Up to that point, you see, I had led a relatively easy life. Schoolwork came naturally. I knew early on that I was interested in pursuing a career in writing, so I never had really struggled with decisions about my future. I didn't play sports so I hadn't done a lot of training or extensive exercise. Truth be told, I had never faced much of an uphill battle in anything . . . till I went up against labor pains. Wow—that was a force to be reckoned with! Still, I'd attended Lamaze classes and knew I didn't want any medication. I was determined I could get through it—and I did!

I came out of that experience exhausted but delighted and also extremely proud. I had pushed myself beyond my limits and knew I was a stronger person because of it.

Getting stronger as life progresses—not weaker—should be our goal. Unfortunately, for some, the process seems to be reversed.

In his book *Finishing Strong*, Steve Farrar talks about some men in the Old Testament who had a great start, but unfortunately did not finish so well. Their names? Shammua, Shaphat, Igal, Palti, Gaddiel, Gaddi, Ammiel, Sethur, Nahbi, and Geuel. You're probably thinking, "Who? I've never heard of them!" (I didn't think I had either.)

The names of their comrades, however, are ones with which we are all familiar: Joshua and Caleb. The previous ten, you see, were among the twelve spies God selected to spy out the land of Canaan. According to Farrar, they were among the Israel's best and brightest—the cream of the crop, so to speak. They had seen the plagues God brought down on Egypt, had witnessed Him open up the Red Sea for His people to cross on dry ground and then close it on top of Pharaoh's army.

They had a great start in life, but then faltered along the way. When it came their time to shine, they buckled. Their faith was weak, and they gave an unfavorable report. Because of their doubt, Israel's possession of the Promised Land was delayed for forty years.

Of course they are not the only ones with that kind of resume. I am sure you can think of those you know personally who began their Christian life with a flourish, only to falter a little further down the road. I can recall a young man at the Christian college I attended. He had begun preaching, I believe, at the ripe old age of 15. By the time he was a freshman in college, his speaking appointments rivaled those of men much older. He graduated and promptly was hired as the pulpit minister for a congregation in a large city. Yet in just a few short years, the promise of that bright life was dimmed. He had divorced and was serving a prison sentence.

What about you? Maybe you had a great start, but one of life's storms has come along and knocked you over. You may be discouraged, even tempted to quit.

Life is a marathon, not a sprint. The following poem reminds us that all we have to do to win is rise each time we fall.

FAITH

*I will not doubt, though all my ships at sea
Come drifting home with broken masts and sails;
I shall believe the Hand which never fails,
From seeming evil worketh good for me;
And though I weep because those sails are tattered
Still will I cry, while my best hopes lie shattered,
"I will trust in Thee."*

*I will not doubt, though all my prayers return
Unanswered from the still, white realm above;
I shall believe it is an all-wise Love
Which has refused those things for which I yearn;
And though at times I cannot keep from grieving,
Yet the pure ardor of my fixed believing
Undimmed shall burn.*

*I will not doubt, though sorrow fall like rain,
And troubles swarm like bees around a hive;
I shall believe the heights for which I strive
Are only reached by anguish and by pain;
And though I groan and tremble with my crosses,
I yet shall see, through my severest losses,
The greater gain.*

I will not doubt; well-anchored in the faith,
Like some staunch ship, my soul braves every gale,
So strong its courage that it will not fail
To breast the mighty unknown seas of Death.
Oh, may I cry, when body parts with spirit,
"I do not doubt," so listening worlds may hear it,
With my last breath.

—*Ella Wheeler Wilcox*

FOR THOUGHT AND DISCUSSION

- Think of some specific examples from the Bible of those who started strong but faltered.

- Think of some Bible examples who finished stronger than they started.

- What are some things you have experienced in your personal life that have made you stronger?

- Eventually storms do subside. But while we are in the midst of them, why does it seem like that time will never come?

- How do you hope to finish life?

Notes

Chapter 12

*"Sunny days seem
to hurt the most
I wear the pain like
a heavy coat."*

—*Kenny Chesney
"Who You'd Be Today"*

A Rainbow Promise

Several years ago, when our second son graduated from college, he decided to spend a year traveling the continental U.S. As he was getting ready to leave, his basketball coach gave him some good advice. He said, "Luke, whenever possible, take the back roads."

Why did he say that? Nowadays we have a wonderful interstate system all across our country. Good roads, well-marked, nearly always the easiest way to get from here to there. But, truth be told, interstate highways are a little impersonal, aren't they? When you're driving along on one, it's almost hard to tell what part of the country you're in. They all look pretty much the same. Coach Champagne was right: you see a lot more of the land, the people, and the places in this country by getting off the beaten track.

In his book, ***The Life God Blesses***, Gordon MacDonald says when he was growing up secondary roads were pretty much the only option for extended travel.

> The secondaries wind through small towns and villages that the interstates avoid, and they usually follow the contours of the countryside. You see things on secondary roads, and so

even though it takes more time and caution, I like to drive them whenever possible.

Now, unlike the interstates, secondary roads do not promise unhindered passage. Sometimes they're poorly maintained, and the ride can be bumpy. Each town seems to have one police officer with a radar unit designed to raise revenues from hapless passersby. And you better be prepared for the inevitable slow-moving vehicle that can keep you crawling for miles along no-passing zones. On the secondaries your ability to predict the exact hour in which you will reach your destination is limited. There are too many potential disruptions along the way.

My personal life has the appearance of travel on one of these secondary roads. A map of the routes I've lived on would show almost no straight lines or freeways anywhere. A log of my life's travels would note experiences reminiscent of detours, accidents, flat tires, potholes, and speeding tickets.

> *We need instructions, and we have them in God's Word. He provides both a map and a guide. And in Him we have someone we can trust because He never changes.*

How we wish that the journey from here to eternity were even and incident-free! But it isn't. There are twists and turns all along the way. Like on a roadway, we would do well to proceed with caution.

The most important thing in this comparison of life to a trip is the importance of asking for and accepting help along the way. We need instructions, and we have them in God's Word. He provides both a map and a guide. And in Him we have someone we can trust because He never changes.

Ever since the time of Noah, the rainbow has symbolized God's promise. I read that astronauts who have been to outer space and seen things from that perspective say that rainbows form a complete circle. Did you know that? I always envisioned them as a half-circle. (No wonder we have never found that pot of gold at the end, right?) God's promises are like that, too—with no break in them.

We as humans can't say that about ourselves. I break my promises even when I don't mean to. I work part-time as a church secretary and sometimes, after services, people will ask me to put an announcement in the bulletin. I mean to do it. But that little piece of paper I write it down on gets lost in the black hole of my pocketbook and I forget. I don't even think about it until they ask me about it the next week. *Oops.*

With God, there is no, "Oops!" Listen to the way Deuteronomy 7:9 is translated in *The Message*: "Know this: God, your God, is God indeed, a God you can depend on. He keeps His covenant of loyal love with those who love Him and observe His commandments for a thousand generations."

We see in the Bible several examples—other than God—of those who kept promises they made. One is Hosea. He loved his wife and took her back time and time again, even when she betrayed him and broke his heart.

And then there is David. Remember the promise he made to his best friend Jonathan? David kept his word. He found crippled Mephibosheth and brought him to the palace, gave him a place at the king's table! He made him a son. (That is a great example of what God has done for us. Mephibosheth did not deserve to be there . . . and we don't either!) Mephibosheth was there because of a promise that endured (1 Samuel 20:14-17,42; 2 Samuel 9).

A woman was taking flying lessons in a small airplane. Her instructor repeatedly reviewed safety procedures. This included the practice of purposefully stalling the aircraft. He would have her pull back on the wheel firmly, steadily climbing, climbing into the air. The plane would eventually shudder, then stall.

Her natural inclination at that moment was to grip the wheel and jerk it back, but her teacher cautioned her against that. He explained that such an action would worsen the stalled condition of the plane and decrease the chances of recovering flight.

Instead, he told her to let go of the wheel completely. The plane was designed so that, with loss of air speed, its nose would tip forward and head toward the earth. This would naturally increase air speed and the plane would level out and fly again. He said the plane was designed to recover *when the pilot let go*.

When I read that story, I thought of how so many times, we cruise along in life at a comfortable speed and altitude. Then, suddenly, we stall. Along come family problems, financial difficulties, sickness, death, and countless other problems. Our natural inclination is to work hard to "fix" things. But the harder we pull on the wheel, the greater our descent into discouragement.

God longs for us to let go and turn things over to Him. "Cast all your anxiety on Him, because He cares for you" (1 Peter 5:7 NIV).

In the verse right before that, He has promised, "Humble yourselves, therefore, under God's mighty hand that He may lift you up in due time" (1 Peter 5:6 NIV).

When is that due time? we wonder. Only God knows. But never doubt that His promises are sure, and the time of lifting up will come.

Problem-free travel may be what we all desire, but in life there is no such thing. Still, with God at the controls, we can weather whatever catastrophes we encounter.

FOR THOUGHT AND DISCUSSION

- Think of some secondary roads you have traveled in life. What life lessons have you learned on them?

- What does it mean to you to know that someone will keep his/her word?

- What reassurance does it give you when that Someone is God?

- There are over 7,000 promises in Scripture. What is one that has special significance to you?

Notes

Chapter 13

"In every situation there is a right way and spiritual way to think. It may take some time to find it. It may take some discipline to embrace it. But it is always there, and it is always best. It is always the key to overcoming any challenge."

—*Tom Jones*

Tying A Knot

A little boy entered a supermarket one day. He asked the grocer where he could find a box of a certain brand of detergent, saying that he needed to wash his cat.

The grocer said, "Son, you shouldn't wash your cat with that kind of soap," but the little boy insisted it would be okay. A few days later, the little boy was in the store again and the grocer asked about his cat. "Oh, he died," the boy replied.

"He died?" the grocer said. "See, I told you not to wash him in that detergent!"

The boy shrugged. "Oh, it wasn't the soap that hurt him. I think it was the spin cycle that did him in."

It is the spin cycles of life that nearly do us in, too. This chapter concludes our discussion of what we are to do when they turn us—as the movie title says—"every which way but loose"!

Several years ago I attended a ladies' day program that had as its theme "What to do when you're at the end of your rope." We have all had those moments, haven't we?

A woman I know had a little boy who was a handful, to say the least. One day she had been at the store buying groceries. When she left the store, she put her purse and keys in the floorboard of her car while she transferred the bags into the backseat. Then she got her little boy out of the buggy and buckled him into his car seat. She turned away for just a second to put the cart away—only two steps from her car—but when she turned back, he had closed the car door and pushed down on the lock. She could not get in! She tried to talk to him through the glass, to coax him to unlock the door, but he just sat there and grinned at her. Then he got into the groceries. First he ate a cookie, but then he opened up the eggs and, one by one, started breaking them (in his hair, all over the seat . . .)! As you can imagine, by this time she was frantic, just about at the end of her rope. She called 911 and told them her keys were locked in her car. They said, "We're sorry, ma'am, but we can't help you with that." She said, "You don't understand. My baby's in the car with my keys . . . and he's got eggs!"

13 SURVIVING A TSUNAMI — Tying A Knot

Calling 911—that's one solution when times are tough. But an even better idea is calling on the Lord.

My friend Cindy Guy says when you are at the end of your rope, you should tie a knot and hang on. Here are ten "NOTS" from Scripture worth hanging onto.

1) Lean NOT on your own understanding (Proverbs 3:5). The first part of this passage says to "trust in the Lord with all your heart." The idea in the original language is to attach oneself as a leech. In other words, be that dependent! Don't rely or prop yourself up on your own understanding of things. Have you ever tried to lean against something that wasn't sturdy? I heard a gentleman tell about being at a church dinner and backing up to a wall which turned out to be one of those portable dividers. He went crashing to the floor, to his great embarrassment! As humans, our understanding of things is not always accurate. We're near-sighted. We're like Paula Prentiss' character in that old,

old movie *Where the Boys Are*—blind as a bat, but too vain to wear her glasses. So she goes around bumping into things and talking to light poles.

2) Let NOT your heart be troubled (John 14:1). Think about what lies ahead and how wonderful it is going to be. The "many rooms" in the next verse in the Greek imply permanent dwelling places. This is a home where we won't have to worry about painting every few years or replacing things that wear out.

3) Walk by faith, NOT by sight (2 Corinthians 5:7). The reason we shouldn't walk by sight is that things aren't always as they appear. Have you ever known anyone to wrap empty boxes and put them under a Christmas tree just to give it a pretty appearance? Satan is masterful at the same type of deception—making things of the world which are actually empty and meaningless look appealing.

4) Despise NOT the chastening of the Lord (Hebrews 12:5). Chastening is unpleasant, but good comes from things that are hard. There is no better example of this than right in my home state of Alabama. We are probably the only place in the world with a monument to a boll weevil! But if it had not been for the boll weevil eating their cotton crops, farmers never would have discovered peanuts. Even out of pain and difficulty, there can be growth and good.

5) It is NOT in man that walketh to direct his steps (Jeremiah 10:23). My mom's favorite thing about our large discount super store is the fact that when you ask clerks where something is located, they don't just tell you, they take you there and show you. It's hard sometimes to find our way on our own . . . in Wal-Mart, and in life!

Imagine turning a group of kindergarten students out on their own and letting them try to find their own way to the gymnasium or bus stop. The results would be disastrous. We are equally clueless in finding our way through life without guidance.

6) Shall we accept good from God and NOT bad? (Job 2:10) Friends of ours adopted a little girl whose growth had been stunted. Her foster parents had been told—incorrectly—that she didn't have long to live, and so they let her eat only what she wanted to eat, which turned out to be sweets all the time. Much as we may love sugar, we know that alone is not a healthy diet. Even so, God knows that a spiritual diet of only good things would not permit us to grow. I read once about a road in London where, in the old days, more horses died traveling than on any other route. Surprisingly, it wasn't a rough, hilly, difficult road, but rather smooth and even. They died because their muscles never developed.

7) God will NOT allow more than we can bear (1 Corinthians 10:13). Sometimes we may

find that hard to believe. He has a lot more confidence in us than we have in ourselves. Author Barbara Johnson has a suggestion for how to bear sorrow when you don't think you can. She says to decide that you are only going to cry for 30 minutes a day. That's going to be the only time you allow yourself to cry, but you're going to do it for half an hour. She says it's amazing how hard it is to actually do when you give yourself permission. Set the timer, put on some sad music, and have at it. The trick is every day to set the timer for one minute less than the day before. By the end of 30 days—or possibly sooner—your crying spells may be over.

8) A threefold cord is NOT quickly broken (Ecclesiastes 4:12). A great example of this principle is in Exodus 17 in the battle against the Amalekites. As long as Moses held up his hands, Israel prevailed. But, as you can imagine, he quickly became tired of holding his hands up in the air. Two friends, Aaron and Hur, helped him out by getting

him a stone on which to sit and then standing on either side of him, helping so that his hands remained steady until the sun set.

9) We do NOT have a high priest who cannot sympathize (Hebrews 4:15). When the son of one of my close friends was in training to be an Army Ranger, his dad went through all the training with him at home (at a much slower pace, of course!). If Dane had to run five miles, that morning before work his dad ran five miles. Whatever we go through—whether it be physical pain, rejection or betrayal by loved ones, ridicule from peers, separation from those we care about—Jesus can relate. He has been through it Himself. In the words of the old hymn "Jesus Knows, Jesus Cares."

10) NOT my will, but Thine be done (Luke 22:42). Jan Karon, in her popular Mitford book series, calls this "the prayer that never fails" and rightly so. This should be our prayer no matter what kind of storm we are facing.

FOR THOUGHT AND DISCUSSION

- What are some other NOTS from scripture that are worth hanging onto?

- Make an acrostic from the word STORM with each letter standing for something good that can come from hardship.

S _____

T _____

O _____

R _____

M _____

Concluding Activity

CONCLUDING ACTIVITY

GRABBING THE MOST IMPORTANT THINGS

- If you had less than five minutes to grab items from all of your suitcases—and still have the ability to run—what would you grab?

- This was a question posed by Rick Von Feldt on his web log in the days following the Asian tsunami.

- Would you know where all of your items were?

What would really matter?

- In the midst of an emotional disaster, just like in a physical one, it is essential to take hold of basics. *Among the things that matter most to me:*

SOURCES

Chapter 1:
    Edwards, Elizabeth. *Saving Graces: Finding Solace and Strength from Friends and Strangers.* New York, New York: Broadway Books, 2006.

Chapter 2:
    Godwin, Gail. *Queen of the Underworld.* New York, New York: Random House, 2006.

Chapter 3:
    King, Cassandra. *Queen of Broken Hearts.* New York, New York; Hyperion, 2007.
    Jeremiah, David. *A Bend in the Road.* Nashville: Word Publishing, 2000.
    Miller, Donald. *Searching for God Knows What.* Nashville: Nelson Books, 2004, page 90. Used with permission.

Chapter 4:
    Calkin, Ruth Harms. Poem used with permission.
    Miller, Donald. *Searching for God Knows What*, page 87. Used with permission.
    Ortberg, John. *If You Want to Walk on Water, You've Got to Get Out of the Boat.* Waterville, Maine: Thorndike Press, 2001, page 181.
    Richmond, Gary. *A View From the Zoo.* Nashville: W Publishing Group, 1987. Used with permission.

Chapter 5:
    Bush, Jenna. *Ana's Story: A Journey of Hope.* New York, New York: HarperCollins, 2007.
    Ortberg, John. *If You Want to Walk on Water, You've Got to Get Out of the Boat,* page 243.
    Yancey, Philip. *The Bible Jesus Read.* Waterville, Maine: Thorndike Press, 1999, pages 109-110.

Chapter 6:
Poem by Adam Lindsay Gordon.

Chapter 7:
Lucado, Max. *Facing Your Giants*. Nashville: W Publishing Group, 2006, page 125.

Chapter 8:
Jeremiah, David. *A Bend in the Road*. Nashville: Word. Publishing, 2000.

MacDonald, Gordon. *The Life God Blesses: Weathering the Storms of Life That Threaten the Soul*. Nashville, Thomas Nelson Publishers, 1994, pages 149-150. Used with permission.

Chapter 9:
Gospel Advocate, September 2007, page 17. Used with permission.

Hellmich, Nanci. "Son's suicide prodded Collins to write," *USA Today*, June 19, 2007, page 7D.

Jeremiah, David. *A Bend in the Road*, page 187.

McMillon, Lynn and Tamie Ross, "A Conversation with Emily Lemley," *Christian Chronicle*, November 2007, page 23. Used with permission.

Miller, Donald. *Searching for God Knows What*, page 58. Used with permission.

"Nature's lessons have been learned the hard way," *USA Today*, September 12, 2005, page 6A.

Chapter 10:
Brestin, Dee. "Don't Send a Sympathy Card," *Focus on the Family Magazine*, July 2007, pages 20-21. Used with permission.

Chapter 11:
Farrar, Steve. *Finishing Strong*. Sisters, Oregon: Multnomah Publishers, 1995, pages 20-21.

Chapter 12:
MacDonald, *The Life God Blesses*, page 24. Used with permission.